Black Cockatoo

This is a Magabala Book

Leading Publisher of Aboriginal and Torres Strait Islander Storytellers.

Changing the World, One Story at a Time.

First published 2018, reprinted 2018 x2, 2019 x5, 2020,
2021 x3, 2022 x2, 2023 x2, 2025 x2, 2026
Magabala Books Aboriginal Corporation
1 Bagot Street, Broome, Western Australia
Website: www.magabala.com Email: sales@magabala.com

Magabala Books is assisted by the Australian Government through Creative Australia, its principal arts investment and advisory body and publishes with support from the WA Government.

Magabala Books is Australia's leading independent Aboriginal and Torres Strait Islander publishing house. We acknowledge the Traditional Owners of the Country on which we live and work. We recognise the unbroken connection to traditional lands, waters and cultures. Through what we publish, we honour all our Elders, peoples and stories, past, present and future.

Cover Design Jo Hunt
Cover Artwork David 'Dub' Leffler
Typeset by Post Pre-press Group
Printed and bound by Griffin Press, South Australia

ISBN (Print) 978-1-925360-70-7
ISBN (ePUB) 978-1-925360-72-1
ISBN (ePDF) 978-1-925360-71-4

NATIONAL LIBRARY OF AUSTRALIA

A catalogue record for this book is available from the National Library of Australia

GOVERNMENT OF WESTERN AUSTRALIA

Australian Government

Creative Australia

Black Cockatoo

by Carl Merrison and Hakea Hustler

Magabala Books

1

The hit came hard, sending the young *dirrarn* black cockatoo reeling from his roost in the large gum tree. The boy approached cautiously, shanghai dangling from his hand, to inspect his catch. The dirrarn lay sprawled amongst the smaller birds he'd been using as target practice.

'Jy! I hope you planning to eat that one, at least,' said Mia, looking at the devastation at the bottom of the yard.

Jy whirled around, shanghai loaded. 'Get lost, nobody asked you.'

Mia bent down, scooped up the dirrarn, cradled it to her chest and walked defiantly back inside, tears in her eyes.

'We don't just kill for the fun of it, *jawiji* grandson,' said Jy's grandfather, as he walked onto the verandah, cup of tea in hand. His calm presence insisted that he be heard.

'Nah, I was just practising, *jawiji* grandfather,' Jy said, head bowed respectfully. 'It was just some fun.'

The grandfather slowly placed his tea on the back table and collected the dead birds from the ground. He threw all except one to the *gunyarr* dogs. 'This one is your dinner,' he said to his grandson. 'Pluck and gut him before you bring him in.'

Jy didn't argue, but when his jawiji walked inside he aimed his shanghai high and shot down a settled *wan.gura* crow from the tree in the neighbour's yard.

Inside the house Mia put the dirrarn into a dark cardboard box. She didn't know what had made her save this one, but she did. Growing up in the bush, she had seen many animals die and had hunted many of her own. She remembered the story her grandmother had told her about this bird, and that culturally she wasn't allowed to say its name or look at it. Seeing the red underwing flash brightly had drawn her attention to the dirrarn's small body sprawled out on the ground. She had been moved and had risked her brother's wrath by picking it up. She wasn't meant to challenge her brother; as her older brother she owed him a certain amount of respect. She wasn't even sure if the bird would survive. She could hear shallow breathing from within the box, so she knew it was alive. She placed the box carefully in her wardrobe, away from prying eyes, and went into the kitchen to join her mother and aunties getting the food ready for dinner.

2

The chorus of the *yidiyidi* cicadas hummed as the family set up the cooking fire in the backyard. Katherine, Mia's mother, threw fresh beef on the hotplate. Jy placed the dead bird next to the other meat cooking on the fire.

As they settled down around the fire waiting for their dinner to cook, Mia's jawiji sat close and began telling a story in a hushed tone.

'Before you were born, Mia, I took your father out hunting. It had been a proper long *barranga* dry weather, so to hunt we didn't have to travel far to find big fat *bin.girrjaru* bush turkey. Your father spotted that bin.girrjaru in the shrub and looked at him. As the spear flew through the air, the breeze caught our smell and that bin.girrjaru took flight, disturbing some dirrarn that were hunting on the ground. The spear hit a dirrarn and killed him. You have his mark, Mia, between your shoulderblades. The dirrarn is your totem. Your *jarriny* totem.'

Mia's hand automatically went to touch the birthmark between her shoulders. She was fascinated; maybe this was why she had been drawn to save the dirrarn and risk so much.

'You shouldn't be saying that bird's name around the children,' Katherine whispered to her father as the family began choosing their food from the hotplate. 'She can't keep him.'

'It was a story she needed to hear, Katherine,' the old man said. 'There is something deep at work here, she will keep it for now.'

'How much big that bite, you big greedy

thing?' Mia's aunty Diane laughed at her from across the fire, as she took a bite of the bin.girrjaru thigh.

'Haha, learnt from the best or what, Aunty?' Mia cheekily replied, pointing to her aunty's stomach. The family burst out laughing.

'And what about you, my son?' asked Diane, as she poked fun at her nephew—he was her sister's son, so culturally he was her son too. 'You will get too muscly eating all that meat. I'm going to have to chase them girls away!'

'Leave room for this one next, jawiji,' said grandfather to Jy as he picked up another piece off the hotplate.

Jy scowled at his grandfather and defiantly bit into the flesh. Sensing the tension, Diane again took up some light-hearted banter. 'What? You only give'm little bit? Looks like fancy French food, that tiny little one! We'll be eating cane toad legs next!'

Katherine, relieved at the change in tone, laughed and joined in the jokes. 'Like you would know, *jij*, sister. You're afraid of flying!'

Mia let her mind wander to all the places she had dreamt of seeing. No one in her family had left the west coast, let alone travelled over oceans. In days past there was no need to, the family had everything they needed on their country. She imagined soaring high above the coastline, red cliffs below, as the waves crashed onto golden shores—even in her imagination she could not fly out over the waves.

As the family finished their feed, large storm clouds rolled in across the horizon and the moon cast eerie shadows as it peeked between the clouds.

'This storm is because of you,' their grandfather said solemnly to Jy. He motioned towards the clouds as a strong wind swirled around the family. 'It's because of the *jiyirr* rainbow bee-eater bird you hunted and the injured dirrarn. You need to respect our past, my jawiji.'

Mia looked to her brother for his reaction—he looked at the clouds and shrugged before walking inside.

The rain soon forced the rest of the family in as well. The power was out so they crowded around the kitchen table to play cards by candlelight.

When Mia returned to her room that night, the dirrarn was sitting in one corner of the room, the box sprawled open on the floor. His wing hung uselessly by his side.

'I know why I saved you now. We are connected, you and I.' She looked at the dirrarn's ruffled but defiant stance—seeing more of herself in the bird than she dared to admit.

'I'll have to find a cage for you tomorrow,' she said to the dirrarn. 'You will be safe in there.'

3

In the morning, Mia looked around for the wounded bird. He was huddled between her chest of drawers and the wall. Tiredly, she remembered that one of her aunties had owned *gulyulyu* budgies before the cheeky neighbourhood boys had killed them in a game with rocks. She was sure her aunt would lend her a cage.

Mia wedged her door shut with a chair before climbing out of her window and carefully leaving it slightly ajar. She didn't want her brother going into her room. Entering the house from the front door, she drew strange looks from her family.

She purposefully wrote a note saying STAY OUT! and stuck it on her bedroom door. No space was really private in her house and she knew her brother would be eager to finish off the dirrarn if he had the chance.

Leaving the house again, Mia walked down the street and through the centre of town to her aunty's house. She called to her aunty from the front yard and her uncle came out. He yelled inside to her aunty, who came out and agreed to lend her the cage. Mia helped her uncle lift it into the back of his ute before he drove her home.

Mia's uncle put the large cage behind the garden shed under the big tree in the backyard so the dirrarn would have privacy and shade. Mia collected a range of leaves, nuts and flowers from the trees in her yard and street, and put them on the bottom of the cage with an ice-cream tub of water. Through the wire she poked the branches low to the cage floor.

Climbing back through her window, Mia found an old T-shirt from a pile of clothes in the corner of the room. She quickly cut it into strips. Quietly, she approached the dirrarn, who silently watched from the corner of the room. He did not like her coming close. Using her knowledge of catching *jarrambayi* sand goanna and other swift little animals, she quickly scooped him up, avoiding his sharp beak and claws. Using the strips of old T-shirt, she tied his wings to his body before walking outside and placing him gently on the cage floor. The dirrarn was eager to be out of her grip and crawled to the corner, staring at her suspiciously.

She needed just one more thing for security.

'Any money, Aunty?' she asked casually of one of the ladies, after heading back inside.

'*Minyan* nothing, what you need money for?' asked an aunt, sharply.

'Come here, granny.' Her grandmother

beckoned to Mia. 'Ignore that cheeky one.' With a sly wink her grandmother dug her wrinkled hands deep into her dress pocket and pulled out some notes. 'You take this and get whatever you want from the shops.'

Mia endured her granny messing up her hair, smiled and walked out. She was on a mission to get to the local shops and back again before an unwelcome visitor noticed and opened the unlocked cage door.

4

The faded, uneven footpath kept Mia's attention as she left her yard and headed towards the shops. A warm wind swept up red dust and threw it lazily on the hot road. A group of boys across the street took turns laughing and playing games with sticks and stones under the patchy shade of an old tree. An uncle beeped the horn of his troopy and waved as he drove by. Mia reached the cool of the shops with relief. She was disappointed to see that her aunty wasn't working, but the grumpy *gardiya* white person was. He watched her carefully as she hunted through the shelves. It was embarrassing. Roger, the shopkeeper, had moved to town decades ago with his wife. His wife had eventually run away from the dust and the heat, and Roger didn't have anywhere else to go—so he never left. Now he was just old and bitter. Mia placed the lock and key on the bench.

'Just that one?' asked Roger.

Mia avoided eye contact and placed the money on the benchtop. Slipping the change into her pocket, Mia was relieved to leave the shop.

Walking back, Mia got a bindi-eye stuck in the side of her foot. She bent down to pull it out, only to receive a blow to the side of her head. She whirled around. Her brother and cousins sat tossing rocks onto the road from the park. They pretended not to acknowledge her but the smirks on their faces gave them away. Mia stuck her middle finger up and quickly jogged out of throwing distance.

Mia was sad. Jy hadn't always been this

way. As she walked, she remembered a time when they had been close. The fun they had had together hunting jarrambayi down the creek bed with the old people; running off together, much quicker than the old people could go and laughing when they snuck out to scare their jawiji—just managing to escape his playful backhand. She thought about the times they had worked on the old quad bike out at their uncle's block—her brother making it run using things she never thought would work—and the times they had explored the bush, just the two of them. Mia thought about the occasions when Jy used to stick up for her at school—wiping her tears and then chasing off the bullies; the times he had come into her room when she'd been crying from a nightmare, holding her until she fell asleep again.

By the time the lock was on the cage, Mia's tears had dried.

5

Mia slept poorly, worrying about the safety of her jarriny as the temperature dropped outside. She didn't exactly know how dirrarn kept warm at night but she imagined them all snuggled together in a flock, or nestled safely in nests. She had snuck outside early, in the still morning, to hang a blanket over the top of the cage to keep in the warmth.

When her grandmother came in to gently shake her awake in the morning, Mia begged for just ten minutes more.

'It's time to get up, Mia,' her grandmother yelled, after what felt like no time. Mia groaned and pulled the blanket over her head.

Mia didn't stir when someone knocked softly on the door.

'Jawiji, you will be late,' Mia's grandfather said gently. She felt the bed dip as he sat down beside her.

'I'm too tired, jawiji.' Mia was tempted to lie and fake sickness. She knew she was never allowed to stay home from school like some kids in her community. There had been nights when the whole family had been up late for one reason or another—a cultural ceremony, a funeral and wake, a relative's birthday party, a sports event, family business. She had never been allowed to use any of those excuses to miss school.

'You will get up now, jawiji,' the old man said sternly, with the authority of her grandfather and Elder. He moved the blanket from her face. 'You know how important learning is.'

As her grandfather got up and closed the door behind him, Mia dragged herself out of bed. She looked in the mirror at the dark bags that framed her dark brown eyes. Slowly she brushed her hair, threw on her favourite pair of jeans and school top.

Mia went into the kitchen. She was thankful that her grandmother handed her two pieces of toast and Vegemite to eat as she walked on her way to school.

6

Mia was happy to see the other students lining up as she walked into the schoolyard. She was relieved she wouldn't have to walk into class late. Mia quickly found her place in line.

The day passed slowly. Mia found it hard to concentrate and focus on what the teacher was trying to teach them. Her mind wandered back to the dirrarn. She wondered where it had come from. *Did the dirrarn's family and flock miss it? Was its wing broken and would it heal?* Mia was aware that the nearest vet was over three hours away in the bigger town.

For her fifth birthday her mother had

given her a puppy. Mia had been so excited and spent every spare hour walking, playing and training her new pup. She had been devastated when the pup had been hit by a car on the street near her home. Even at a young age, Mia had known something was wrong when her grandfather brought the pup in, wrapped in his jacket. Her grandmother had placed the pup in a cardboard box lined with warm towels, and the box was left by Mia's bed overnight, so that she could handfeed and comfort him. When the pup had not recovered by morning, Mia begged her grandparents to make the long trip into town to get help. Mia remembered stroking the puppy's thick brown fur as he rested on her lap and whimpered during the drive. The pup did not make it halfway.

Mia knew she had less chance of convincing any family member to pay for a visit to the vet for a bush bird. There was so much she loved about her Country. But sometimes she wanted . . . more.

Mia was glad when the bell went for lunch and more so when her grandmother dropped off a packed lunch at the office. She sat at the end of the oval eating her sandwich under the shade of a large tree, watching her friends practise their handstands on the soft grass. The school groundskeeper took pride in ensuring the oval was always lush and green.

Mia's gaze rested on Jy and his mates, along the oval boundaries. She noticed them catching *birlbirlji* grasshoppers. She saw the boys draw lines in the patches of loose red dirt by the school fence. She winced as she realised that they were pulling off the wings of the birlbirlji and forcing them to jump on the hot dust. Without thinking, Mia touched the birthmark between her shoulder blades and felt bad for the little insects suffering and their sudden loss of freedom. She was relieved when a teacher saw them, told them all off and sent them on their way.

7

That afternoon Mia sat peeling potatoes with her grandmother out on the verandah. The heat of the day had yet to disappear and the gentle breeze provided welcome relief. She watched her grandfather carving a boomerang under the large old tree, his soft humming reaching her ears. Mia was grateful that she still had her grandparents from her mother's side. She hadn't seen her father's family since she was a toddler. Now she was older, she wondered what their Country was like. She wondered what anywhere other than *here* was like. *Where had the dirrarn's adventures taken it? Had it travelled across red deserts to the golden sands of the East? Had it seen the huge ocean cliffs to the cold south?* Mia loved her Country, but sometimes she wondered if there was more.

'When I was little, my old people taught us our language, culture and all about our Country, *jaja* granddaughter,' her grandmother said, as her hands rhythmically peeled potatoes. 'That was all we needed. Things are different now.' She paused. 'It was good you went to school today.'

Mia continued to watch her grandfather working and the dirrarn basking in the dying light. She listened respectfully and allowed a thoughtful silence.

'You live in both worlds,' her grandmother added. 'You will be strong both ways.'

Mia didn't reply. Sometimes she wished that she lived in a time when her ancestors were here. It was hard code-switching, always trying to get things right both ways. Maybe that's why her brother was having such a hard time? Maybe he just gave up?

Even as she thought of him, a football bounced over their fence. Jy walked into the yard. Mia noticed her grandfather's face light up. He motioned to the tools and spare wood around him.

'My mates are waiting, jawiji,' Jy laughed. 'I'll buy you a finished one from the tourist centre!'

Mia's heart broke for her grandfather . . . and for her brother.

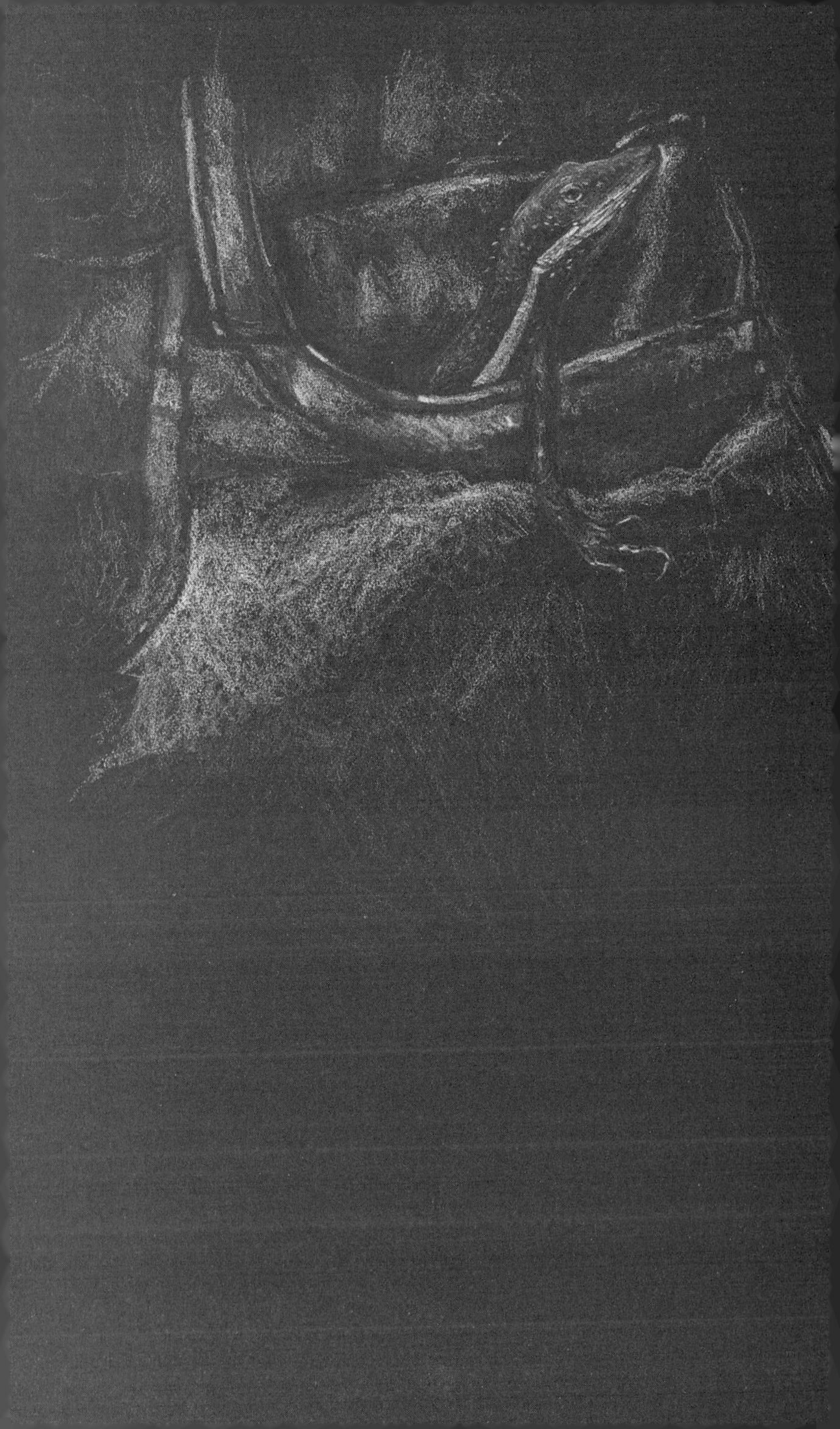

8

The weeks went by and the dirrarn gained physical strength, but his mind was still broken. He walked from one side of the cage to the other and constantly chewed on the corner wire.

In the mornings before the family woke, other dirrarn gathered in the trees. They took turns landing beside his cage and copying his sad dance.

Jy sometimes came outside to puff on a smoke that he had pocketed from his grandfather. Sometimes it was the *mangirrigirri* tata lizard he was hunting—hiding them in his pockets to take to school to frighten his teachers. Occasionally, it was the newly arrived cane toad—grabbing them by their legs and picking a stick off the ground to hit them across the yard like a tennis ball.

At night, occasionally, the silence was broken by the laughter of the family as they sat around outside eating *marlu* kangaroo or jarrambayi fresh off the fire. Other times, it was broken by loud music, the songs from the old people as they sat on the back porch, or the quiet crying of Mia who was worried by the sounds of relations arguing.

One day, Mia was slow to return home from school—her cousin-sisters had persuaded her to join them for a swim at the town pool. Afterwards, with her hair still wet from the swim, Mia walked into the yard, ready to fill up the water in the cage. As she rounded the garden shed, she stopped. Jy and an older cousin, Tobias, were kneeling by the cage, smiles plastered across their faces. Mia watched as Jy guided the end of a thin, scaly tail through the bars.

She screamed and ran. Driving her shoulder into her brother's stomach, she bumped him aside. Groping for the key that was on a string around her neck, she kneeled at the cage door. Tobias grabbed her by her shoulders, yanked her up and locked her arms behind her back. She kicked out as Jy stood up. The *murnduj* black-headed python sniffed the air with its tongue. The dirrarn squawked and climbed higher up the branches in the cage. Jy turned towards her, anger in his eyes. Tobias laughed. She held her breath. The back door banged open.

'Stop!' shouted their grandfather. 'Enough fighting. You should feel shame fighting your sister.'

The grip loosened and Mia quickly dropped to her knees by the cage; lock off. She wasn't afraid of the python and easily grabbed it by its neck and threw it out into the grass. With the bird safe, she lowered her head in relief.

Jy seethed, his anger rippled under his scarred skin—the skin of a fifteen year old who had grown up hard in the red-ground country. Mia, her skin unblemished, radiated optimism and hope.

The grandfather watched Tobias run off out of the yard. He then turned to face his grandson, who stared defiantly back at him, veins popping in his arms, down to his clenched fists. The old man met his gaze sadly, his disappointment clear. Jy broke the stand-off, bowed his head and stormed back into the house.

9

Late that night, Mia woke feeling thirsty. She walked bleary-eyed into the kitchen to get a drink. As she sipped the cool water, she heard her grandparents' voices in the lounge room.

'I'm worried for him.' Mia could hear the helplessness in her grandfather's voice. 'I am not young enough to catch him and growl him anymore.'

Mia remembered when her grandfather could easily catch Jy for a stern word or a soft clip around the ear to remind him of his behaviour. Mia remembered laughing at her brother's bad luck at getting caught for whatever mischief they had been up to together. Now, Jy no longer sat eagerly waiting to hear his jawiji's tales, advice or creation stories about the land and languages they were all connected to. Mia was a little shamed to think that she hadn't done that much lately either.

'I'm just tired,' her jawiji's voice continued. 'You and I have lived through so much. I'm not sure I have it in me to teach him the right ways anymore. He is just so headstrong.'

'Proper stubborn like you,' said Mia's jaja, laughing softly.

Mia knew only snippets of her grandparents' life. Her jawiji had been born out bush and had spent much of his childhood living the traditional way. He told stories of those days when they had fished down at the waterhole. The taste of fresh fish often brought back his memories.

Jawiji had met Mia's jaja on the station when they were teenagers. Her family had been rounded up and forced to live there. Jaja rarely talked about the little sister her family had lost when the government and police rounded up the lighter-skinned kids. On the rare occasion she did, the pain was raw in her words and plain across her face.

Mia's grandmother had been born and raised on that station. She told Mia many stories of how she had later found her culture and connection; one that had been taken from her family when they were forbidden to speak their language. So much had happened in her grandparents lifetimes, and now old age and family worries wearied them.

Mia worried for their health, and she was also well aware that Jy had slowly lost respect for his grandfather and family. Weekend trips out bush or family gatherings had gradually changed to Jy hanging out with mates and being cheeky. If only he could turn his anger into passion, Mia felt that it could make a difference.

'I wish Jy would just go out to the station when his uncles ask him,' Mia heard her jawiji continue. Mia knew how hard her uncles and cousin-brothers worked the land. They all took pride in it. These men could rival any townsfolk, even with their more modern vehicles and equipment. Her relations knew the land like they knew how to breathe. Mia's jawiji had taught his sons long ago to stand strong in the knowledge of their culture, language and land.

Mia's head reeled. She couldn't listen any longer. With a heavy heart and a mind full of worry, she crept back to bed to try to sleep.

10

The next day, when Mia woke, she heard voices out on the front verandah. She walked out bleary-eyed and was excited to see her uncles and cousin-brothers from the station.

'How's my young mum doing?' her older cousin's son Chris asked, shooting her a bright smile. His hair had grown wild from months out bush.

'All good here,' Mia replied. 'Bring me any bush honey, or what?' Chris laughed and the deep sun-wrinkles that framed his dark brown eyes smiled with him. 'That's all you need me for, hey?' Out of his backpack he pulled an old coffee jar, full with *sugarbag* bush honey. Mia's mouth watered.

'You think you the only countryman that can bring Mia bush treasure, unks?' said her cousin-brother Scotty playfully as he elbowed Chris out of the way. 'What you think of this, cuz?'

Mia unwrapped the muslin cover to find a cold, sharp rock, long and almost diamond-shaped.

'What is it?' Mia hadn't seen anything like it before, yet it felt comfortable and familiar in her hands.

'That's an old spearhead. Our ancestors would have used that one out hunting. We found it near the cliff face at one of our new fishing spots, further out bush,' Scotty replied with an excited glint in his eyes. 'Whole lot of old stuff there like that. Proper eerie, standing on country that our mob haven't been back on for that long. Dad reckons he went there a bit with his old people when he was young, before the gardiyas came and rounded 'em up onto reserves.'

'Can you take me out there one day?' asked Mia. Her heart ached slightly and she couldn't place the feeling. Maybe it was longing for connection? Maybe it was sadness at what had been lost? 'Can I keep it?'

'It's yours, cuz,' Scotty said as he folded her fingers over the spearhead. 'I reckon we can get some of the old people to take us all out there one time, do it all proper way, you know?'

'Enough spoiling her, you mob,' Rosa, Mia's jaja, said, popping her head around the front door. 'Get in here and sit down for a cuppa. You've got stories to tell us, no doubt!'

Mia's uncles settled down on the sofa while her cousin-brothers eagerly sat around the kitchen table eating the sandwiches Rosa had whipped up.

'You all high-class now, Mia-moo?' Scotty teased. 'Jawiji told us you been and got yourself accepted into some fancy school down south?'

'I'm not sure if I'll go yet,' Mia replied. Her heart filled with indecision every time she thought about it.

'Don't worry, Mia, I'll be the favourite grandkid 'till you get back,' Chris teased, giving his grandmother a quick squeeze.

'Scotty, what you reckon, bi?' laughed Mia. 'He got anything on you?'

'I know I'm deadly. Chris saw me with that snake last week. I'm proper bush warrior now!' replied Scotty, as he acted out his battle with the snake. The whole family couldn't stop laughing as he wriggled around on the floor.

'What you mob in town for this time?' Mia asked. It wasn't unusual to see some of her cousin-brothers come in to get supplies or to see that side of the family in town at rodeo time or for a funeral.

'We've come to drag your brother and jawiji out with us! It's Law time,' Chris replied, taking a huge bite from his sandwich. Jy hadn't been out bush much with family lately. He chose to hang with his mates down at the oval or basketball courts late into the night. Mia had lain in bed most nights, listening to her mother talking to her grandmother in the lounge room, worrying about what had become of her son.

Mia's thoughts were interrupted. 'You bring my husband back safe,' said Rosa. 'He forgets his body has grown old!' Rosa made a point of pulling on some of her husband's grey hair before turning to her grandson. 'Be safe.'

Mia could see Jy's mouth move to object as his eyes met his grandmother's and then softened. He slumped, bowed his head and walked into his room to pack some clothes in his backpack. Jawiji's duffel bag was by the door. A respected Law man, he knew the seasons and signs and had been patiently waiting to head out bush. Mia guessed he had 'forgotten' to tell Jy so that his cousin-brothers could persuade him in person and to avoid another confrontation. Everyone knew you just needed to bundle a few clothes in a bag for any trip out bush with the family. Everyone was good at getting bush food, digging soaks and sleeping under the stars.

Mia laughed with her uncles as they waited for her brother to come out. Soon enough jawiji got up, left the house and settled himself in the front passenger seat of the ute. The younger men jumped in the back. Mia wished she was going out hunting and wondered how long it would be until they returned this time.

‘You got any promise husband, Mia?’ Chris teased. ‘Or do we have to chase all those boys away from you while we in town?’

‘Shut up, Chris!’ Mia laughed. ‘You boys are sick. I don’t need no boy humbug here! I got my own dreams, ’ey?’

‘Too right! You got too many cousin-brothers for any boy to get brave enough to ask you out anyway!’ Scotty laughed.

‘Let’s get on the road, you lot, before the sun goes down and those roos come out!’ jawiji yelled. Jy jumped on the back to join his cousin-brothers. Mia’s uncle Ralph turned the ignition and country music blasted from the stereo. With a toot of the horn they were off. Mia waved goodbye, and knew that some of the boys would return as men.

11

That afternoon Mia sat out by the big tree talking to the dirrarn in his cage. Jawiji had not been able to heal the bird with the veterinary skills he had learnt, nor had her jaja been able to help with bush medicine. Mia felt helpless.

The dense shade of the old tree and a light breeze provided relief from the heat. Mia soon became tired and rested her head on one of the large knotted tree roots that wove its way through the grass. Soon Mia fell asleep.

Mia dreamt she was flying. She had a sense of freedom and felt the force of the wind under her wings. She saw many places over vast distances: the red-lined rises of giant worn mountains; round large boulders that dotted the landscape; the rich, green path of swollen riverbeds. She enjoyed the freedom and the company of her kind as they rested in trees and soared on the breeze. Mia laughed wildly with them by waterholes and kept a respectful distance between herself and her fellow winged beings. She also flew higher into the sky as the red sun warmed her feathers.

Slowly, Mia began to spiral down and landed with a gentle thud. Wire dimmed the sunlight, making a sad patchwork shadow on the pindan floor. She felt worried and her limbs ached. Mia felt dirt underfoot, compacted from the constant walking to and fro. Mia woke with a start, and finally understood.

Mia stared at her captive. She gently reached into the cage, carefully avoiding the strong beak and sharp claws. Slowly Mia untied the cloth strips that held the wings in place. She watched as the dirrarn slowly stretched his fragile wings. She knew he would not last long in the bush, outside the safety of his cage, but Mia knew it was right. She left the cage door open, gave a silent nod and walked away. A strong wind stirred up red dust around her and she could feel the dirrarn's freedom.

Mia looked around *her* cage—the red dirt yard, her family home, her street, her town. She wondered about her freedom as she continued to walk. At the end of town, she heard it—the beautiful wailing of a familiar voice. Mia followed the singing into the bush. In language, she could hear her aunty telling the story of the dirrarn. The voice wove the tale into the air, connecting and freeing Mia with her words.

Mia realised that freedom was in her, her land and her soul. She understood she could stretch her wings far and still land safely back home whenever she needed. Wherever she went.

A strong wind blew around Mia and she could feel freedom like a physical force.

Glossary

Jaru

Barranga – late dry season and build-up to the wet, which is the best time to hunt bush turkey

Bin.girrjaru – bush turkey

Birlbirlji – grasshopper

Dirrarn – red-tailed black cockatoo; when seen in large numbers the cockatoos tell locals the rains are coming

Gulyulyu – budgerigar

Gunyarr – dog

Jaja – grandmother/granddaughter; a respectful term of address used by both members of the pair (see Jawiji)

Jarrambayi – sand goanna

Jarriny – conception totem

Jawiji – grandfather/grandchild; a respectful term of address used by both members of the pair

Jiyirr – rainbow bee-eater

Mangirrigirri – tata dragon lizard

Marlu – kangaroo

Minyan – nothing

Murnduj – black-headed python

Wan.gura – crow

Yidiyidi – cicada

Aboriginal English/Kriol

Bi – slang term meaning 'eh?'

Cuz – slang term for cousin

Feed – food

Gardiya – white person

Guts – belly

Jij/jija – sister

Shanghai – slingshot

Sugarbag – bush honey

Unks – slang term for uncle

Young mum – an aunty on a mother's side of the family, who is younger than the niece or nephew

Carl Merrison is a Jaru and Kija man from Halls Creek in the Kimberley. Footy is his passion and he worked at the Clontarf Foundation for ten years mentoring boys, and coaching the local footy team. Carl was a 2016 WA Local Hero Finalist. Carl was inspired to write about his life growing up in a remote town.

Hakea Hustler is a teacher that loves nature, reading and writing. These passions led her to teach and volunteer in remote communities and rural schools. She has lived all over Australia. She was inspired by the colourful stories her students shared as well as many of the unique problems young people in the outback face.